CRÊPES

SIMPLE. SCRUMPTIOUS. STYLISH.

Acknowledgements and Thank You!

When writing the contemporary romance novel Momentous Kisses, I (Jessica Gray) researched breakfast crêpe recipes and found the website www.world-of-crepes.com.

If you have read Momentous Kisses you may remember that Allison made breakfast crêpes for Russel. Crêpes Croque Madame and Crêpes with Strawberries to be exact.

I immediately fell in love with those wonderful crêpe recipes, and my family did, too. Long after the novel was published I came back to find more crêpe recipes, this time not for research, but to devour.

I teamed up with Christine to bring you this delightful recipe book, which I hope you will enjoy as much as we do. Thank you so much for being such a wonderful reader!

If you ever want to reach us, you can do so via Facebook, Twitter or Email.

Contact Jessica

If you'd like to get in touch with me you can do so via
Twitter:
http://twitter.com/author_jessica

Facebook:
http://facebook.com/jessicagrayauthor

Email:
jessicagrayauthor@gmail.com

Contact Christine

Email:
christine@world-of-crêpes.com

Website: http://www.world-of-crêpes.com

—

2

Copyright

Table of Contents

INTRODUCTION

Tools to Make Crêpes

When making crêpes, what kind of pan do you need?

While you can cook
pancakes free-form on a
large griddle, you do
need a pan to make
crêpes because the batter
is much thinner.

A pan with a defined
edge is necessary to
control the size and
thickness of the crêpe.

The ideal pan for making crêpes will be 8 or 10 inches in diameter.

What is the best material for a crêpe pan?

The jury is out on what material
is best. It all depends on your
comfort and proficiency level.

The 10″ blue steel crêpe pan
(pictured above) is the pan used
by experienced crêpe chefs.

It is made of cold, rolled steel and
is sometimes referred to as black
steel pan.

The design has changed very little since the 1600s. It's a thin pan with a
very shallow rim, and a long, slim handle.

This pan does need to be lightly greased. I usually brush it with a oil or
butter before making the first crêpe, that this is plenty for making a batch
of up to 10 crêpes. The pan I use is made by a company in France called
DeBuyer.
http://www.world-of-crepes.com/best-crepe-pan.html

It is not necessary, however, to use a special crêpe pan. Traditional all-
purpose non-stick pans make excellent crêpe pans for beginners.

Mixing Bowl or Blender

Another tool you will need is either a blender or mixing bowl to mix your batter. An electric blender is the easiest to use because it can whirl your batter at the push of a button, but it is not necessary at all.

To the left is my favorite mixing bowl, which is 7" wide and 5" deep.
When you mix your batter by hand, you will need a whisk to ensure a smooth consistency.

Read my review about the best blenders to use here: http://www.world-of-crepes.com/best-blender-reviews.html

Spatula

To turn your crêpe, you may use a spatula (as pictured) or a wooden crêpe turner that comes with many crêpe-making kits.

I prefer a long pancake spatula, as pictured. Of course, the true experts need no tool at all. They can flip the crêpe by hand.

Perfect Crêpes–Every Time

1 Place your preferred pan on a medium-hot burner. Once hot, brush with a little oil or butter. Remove any excess by blotting lightly with a paper towel. If you have too much grease on your pan, your first crêpe will "fry".

2 Pour 2-3 tbsp of batter (I use a ¼ measuring cup) onto pan. Using wrist, swirl batter until it completely covers the bottom of the pan.

3 Return pan to burner. As the crêpe cooks, a thin, crisp edge will form.

Generally, depending on the heat of your stove and the pan itself, it will take about 1-2 minutes before crêpe is ready to be flipped.

4 Nudge the edge of the crêpe with the spatula. If the crêpe is dry and does not stick, it is ready to be flipped.

This is what the reverse of the crêpe will look like when it is ready to flip. If the underside of your crêpe is golden brown, flip it.

5 Let your crêpe cook for an additional 15-30 seconds at most.

6 *Note:* Because crêpe batter is so thin, by the time you flip your crêpe it is nearly cooked. So the second side will never take as long to cook as the first.

7 When your crêpe is cooked, the second side will also be dry and "polka dots" may appear. See the picture below for an idea of how your second side will appear.

8 Repeat with remaining batter. Stack each crêpe between a sheet of waxed paper, parchment paper, or tin foil until you're ready to use it.

Cover the stack with a dishtowel to keep them warm if you plan to eat them very soon. Or, you may freeze the entire stack for later (for up to 6 months).

After you've refrigerated your batter for at least 30 minutes, be sure and give it another whisk or whirl in the blender. This step helps thoroughly redistribute the flour and makes sure that the first crêpe to the last is consistent in thickness.

If you make crêpes as much as we do, you'll love this time-saving shortcut. If you're planning to make a baked crêpe recipe, it is only necessary to cook the first side of the crêpe. They actually roll up a little easier if they're softer.

Want to serve crêpes in the morning but you know you'll be rushed? Mix your batter the night before. Just be sure and warn your late-night refrigerator prowlers. At night, crêpe batter looks remarkably similar to a vanilla smoothie!

Not sure if your pan is hot enough? Drop one scant teaspoon of crêpe batter onto your pan. If it sizzles and turns into a "mini-crêpe" almost instantly, your pan is ready!

Food storage expert Kim Henke suggests that crêpes can be an elegant and delicious solution to leftovers: "If you've made too much jam, make a batch of crêpes and enjoy them for breakfast or dessert with a generous smear of jam and a sprinkling of powdered sugar."

Planning to make a batch of crêpes ahead of time? While we usually recommend stacking waxed paper between your crêpes as you make them, if you're planning to make them ahead of time and reheat later, place a sheet of tin foil in between each crêpe to keep them from sticking.

To reheat, simply place the bundle in a 325-degree oven for about 10 minutes.

Seven Reasons to love Crêpes

1. They are so sweet

Who can resist, when the smell of freshly baked dough combines with the fragrance of chocolate, sweet fruits and nuts? Have a crêpe as main dish or dessert and feel like you've gone to heaven.

2. Eat a savory crêpe for dinner

If you prefer it savory, crêpes are for you, too. There are a huge variety of recipes for the sophisticated taste: Vegetarian, Meat Lover or Connoisseur of Fish.

3. Delicious Fingerfood

Bring your mini crêpes to the next potluck party. Small bite-sized pieces, rolled with salmon or ham.

4. They taste cold as well as warm

Crêpes will find a place in every lunch box and make the perfect romantic picnic.

5. They are healthy

Combine the batter with veggies, fruits, or nuts and you'll have a healthy snack.

6. Kids love them

I have yet to meet a kid who doesn't devour a crêpe. Spoil them with the sweet ones and give them the savory crêpes for lunch or dinner.

7. They are fast and easy to prepare

It doesn't take hours of preparations. A crêpe can be on the table within minutes.

Basic Crêpe Batter

Every great crêpe recipe starts with a basic recipe for batter. This foolproof recipe will work beautifully for nearly every recipe in this book. The exceptions (our chocolate and fruity batters) — are noted.

Makes 8-10 eight-inch crêpes

- ¾ cup of all-purpose flour
- 1 tbsp of melted butter
- 1¼ cups of skim milk
- 2 eggs
- ¾ tsp of salt

1 Combine all ingredients into a blender and mix until well-blended. If combining by hand, mix the eggs and milk separately and combine slowly with the dry ingredients.

2 Mix in the melted butter last.

3 *Important*: Refrigerate the batter for at least 30 minutes. This gives the batter the opportunity to rest and fully come together.

Chocolate Crêpe Batter

Crêpe batter recipe with a twist: Use dark chocolate to make the most amazing batter for your dessert crepes

Makes 12 eight-inch crêpes

- 2 oz. of semisweet chocolate (morsels or bar chocolate)
- 1 cup of milk
- ½ cup of half and half
- 2 tbsp of cocoa powder
- 1 tbsp of sugar
- 1 cup of all-purpose flour
- 2 eggs

1 Heat milk gently in a small saucepan. Add chocolate. Stir gently until chocolate is completely melted.

2 Combine chocolate-milk mixture and remaining ingredients into blender and process until smooth.

3 Refrigerate for 30 minutes.

Wild Berry Batter

Studded with puréed blueberries and raspberries, this crepe batter recipe is also healthy.

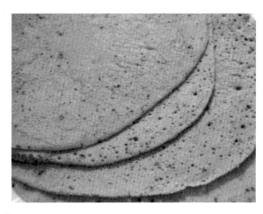

Makes 18 eight-inch Crêpes

- 1½ cups all-purpose flour
- tablespoons melted butter
- 1¾ cups skim milk
- eggs
- 1 tablespoon granulated sugar
- ¼ cup off fresh or frozen mixed berries (We used a combination of small Maine blueberries and raspberries)
- pinch of salt

1 Combine all ingredients except for frozen fruit into a blender and mix until well-blended.

2 Add the fruit at the end and purée until smooth.

3 Important: Refrigerate the batter for at least 30 minutes. This gives the batter the opportunity to rest and fully come together.

Use Quality Ingredients

Flour
Our recipes call for all-purpose flour. But once you have some experience, you can experiment with different flours. Spelt, rye, soy flour, all of them can be use to make crêpe batter.

Eggs
Use medium sized eggs.

Butter
Is the best ingredient, but you have to be careful not to heat it too much. All recipes in this book call for unsalted butter.

Water
Sprinkle some mineral water into your batter and it will become fluffier and the crêpes turn out crispier.

Milk
Always use full cream milk. With skim milk you won't get a satisfactory batter and the taste is flat.

Sugar
If not otherwise noted, we use white sugar, because it because it dissolves the fastest. But you can also use honey or syrup. You'll need to experiment with the amount, though.

SAVORY CRÊPES

Mexican Crepas de Pollo

Mexican Crêpes are called crepas and this one is filled with chicken and a delightful green sauce.

4 Servings

- 1 medium onion, finely chopped
- 2 tbsp of butter
- 1 tbsp dates, chopped
- 2 medium tomatoes, peeled, seeded and chopped
- ¼ cup of pine nuts, toasted
- 2 large chicken breasts, cooked and diced
- 1 tbsp of Spanish olives, chopped
- 2 jalapeno peppers, finely chopped
- 4 basic crepes

1 First, prepare your crêpes. Set aside.

2 Prepare the filling. Sauté the onions in the butter until soft. Add the tomatoes and simmer for five minutes.

3 Add remaining ingredients and simmer for five more minutes. Remove the pan from the heat. Place ⅓ cup of filling in each crêpe, roll into a tube, and lay in a buttered baking dish.

4 Make the sauce. Lightly brush the chilies with oil and place under the broiler until singed on all sides. Wrap them in a damp towel, and allow to rest for approximately 30 minutes.

5 Remove the stems and seeds from the peppers. Sauté the peppers and the onions in butter until the onions become translucent.

6 Place onions and peppers into a blender, and purée until smooth. Return mixture to pan. Mix cornstarch with milk; add to the pepper and onion mixture; simmer gently for approximately 5 minutes.

7 Add ¼ cup of grated cheese and stir until incorporated evenly. Pour sauce over the crêpes and sprinkle with remaining cheese. Bake in 350-degree oven for 10 min. Remove and garnish with chopped cilantro.

Beef Burgundy Crêpes

A meal filling your house with the flavors of old-world France

4 – 8 servings

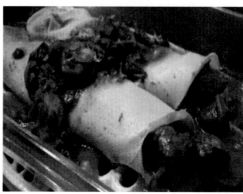

- 6 oz. bacon
- 3-5 tbsp olive oil
- 3-4 tbsp butter
- 1 large sweet onion
- 3 cups beef broth
- 2 lbs. stew beef
- 1 bay leaf
- 3 tbsp all-purpose flour
- 3 cups full-bodied red wine such as Cabernet Sauvignon or burgundy
- ½ tsp coarse black pepper
- 3 tbsp fresh chopped parsley or 1½ tbsp dried parsley
- ½ tsp sugar
- 1 lb. fresh button mushrooms, sliced
- ½ tsp of orange zest
- 8 basic crêpes

1 Cook bacon on medium heat until crisp, reserving 3-4 tbsp of fat. Set aside the bacon and drain. Crumble bacon and save for garnish.

2 Next, brown beef stew in bacon drippings and set aside. Sauté onion using as much oil as needed. Continue cooking until the onion is caramelized and adding sugar, which will help caramelize the onion.

3 Add onions, zest, broth and wine as well as beef, pepper, and bay leaf to a 6-8 quart stockpot. Simmer for 2½ to 3½ hours on low heat. The beef should be tender and the liquid should be reduced by one-half.

4 Melt butter. Add flour and sauté on medium heat until thoroughly mixed. Add this mixture to thicken the stew. Then remove from heat. Sauté mushrooms on medium heat until golden brown and set aside.

5 Preheat oven to 350°. Divide beef mixture among the crêpes, roll up and place inside oiled casserole dish. Cook until edges of crêpes begin to brown (about 10 minutes). Serve 1-2 crêpes per person with mushrooms, crumbled bacon and a little parsley on top.

Seafood Crêpes

Shrimp, fish, and scallops in a savory tomato-saffron sauce.

4 – 8 servings

- 4 tbsp of butter
- 4 tbsp of olive oil
- 1 medium onion, diced
- 8 oz. of mushrooms
- 5 tbsp of flour
- 16 oz. can of diced tomatoes, drained
- ⅛ tsp of chili powder
- Pinch of saffron
- Pinch of white pepper
- 1 tsp Old Bay or Cajun seasoning
- 3 cups of seafood or vegetable broth
- 2 cups of clam juice
- 1 cup of firm white fish (such as orange roughy or Alaskan pollock) cut into ¾-inch pieces
- 1 cup of de-veined shrimp, tails removed
- 1 cup of bay scallops or quartered sea scallops
- basic crêpes

1 Melt butter and olive oil in a 4-quart medium stockpot. Sauté onion and mushrooms for 3-5 min or until vegetables soften and caramelize.

2 Sprinkle flour on vegetables and stir until flour is completely incorporated, about 1-2 minutes. Add broth, juice, tomatoes, and seasonings. Reduce heat and let simmer for 30 minutes. Taste broth and adjust seasonings, adding a little salt or more pepper as desired.

3 Meanwhile, make basic crêpes. If you made your crêpes ahead of time, wrap them in foil and reheat in a 325-degree oven for about 10 minutes or until warmed.

4 Add fish, shrimp, and scallops and cook 3-5 minutes, or until seafood is no longer opaque.

5 Lay first crêpe flat on the serving dish. Spread ½ cup of shrimp, fish and scallops inside. Roll up and cover with 1-2 tablespoons of sauce. Repeat with remaining crêpes. Garnish with minced chives of parsley.

Chicken Divan Crêpes

This recipe starts with simple ingredients such as frozen broccoli and cream of chicken soup. In our household, we call it "Chicken Divine!"

4 – 8 servings

- 2 ½ cups diced or shredded cooked chicken
- 3 cups of frozen broccoli cuts, thawed and drained
- 1 cup of mild cheddar cheese, divided
- 2 cans of cream of chicken soup
- ⅔ cup of milk

- ¼ cup bread or cracker crumbs
- ¼ cup chopped fresh parsley
- ½ tsp of salt
- ¼ tsp of black pepper
- 1 tbsp of melted butter
- 8 basic crêpes

1 Preheat oven to 400°. Stir together, salt, pepper, milk and ½ cup of cheese in a large bowl. Combine well. Scoop out 1 cup of the soup mixture and set aside.

2 Add chicken and broccoli to the remaining mixture and stir together.

3 Lay first crêpe flat on a flat working surface. Spoon ½ cup of the chicken-broccoli mixture inside and roll up. Lay the crêpe inside an oiled 9" x 13" casserole dish. Repeat with the remaining crêpes.

4 Spread the reserved soup mixture down the middle of the crêpes and along the sides. Spread the remaining cheese across the middle and top with the bread or cracker crumbs. Pour melted butter over top of crumbs.

5 Bake for 20-25 minutes until the cheese melts and crêpes are bubbling and golden brown. Sprinkle with parsley and serve immediately.

Welsh Rarebit Crêpes

If you like the delicious combination of beer and cheese, you're certain to enjoy it broiled over crêpes!

4 servings

- 1 cup of dark beer
- 1 cup of heavy cream
- 3 cups of extra sharp cheddar cheese
- 4 egg yolks
- 1½ tbsp of Worcestershire sauce
- 1 tsp of dry mustard
- ½ tsp of salt
- Dash of hot sauce
- 4 slices of fresh tomato
- 8 basic crêpes

1 Boil beer in a small saucepan until reduced by half, about 3 minutes. Next, add the cream and reduce the entire mixture to ¾ cup (about 3 minutes). Remove from heat.

2 Pour into a bowl and let cool to room temperature. Add cheese, egg yolks, Worcestershire sauce, hot sauce, mustard, and salt.

3 Cover a baking sheet with tin foil and preheat broiler. Fold each crêpe in half and then over again, into a triangle. Stack two triangles on top of each other, place on baking sheet and repeat with remaining crêpes. You will have four sets of two crêpes each.

4 Spread each stack with a ¼-inch layer of Welsh Rarebit sauce. Repeat with remaining crêpes.

5 Broil until sauce is golden brown and bubbly. Remove form heat and top with 1 slice of tomato. Serve immediately.

Lobster Newburg Crêpes

Based on the classic creamy Lobster Newburg dish, this crêpe recipe is truly deluxe.

4 servings

- 3 egg yolks
- 1 cup of half and half
- 3 tbsp of sherry
- 2 tbsp of butter
- ¼ tsp of chili powder
- ½ tsp of salt
- ¼ tsp of white pepper
- cups of lobster tail meat, 4 cooked and diced into ½-inch pieces
- 4 basic crêpes

1 First, make your crêpes. If you made your crêpes ahead of time, wrap them in foil and reheat in a 325-degree oven for about 10 minutes or until warmed.

2 Meanwhile, beat egg yolks in a medium bowl. Add half-and-half, sherry, and seasonings. Set aside.

3 Melt butter in a medium saucepan over low heat. Add egg-cream mixture. Stir to combine and bring to a simmer. Simmer for 4-6 minutes, stirring occasionally, until sauce thickens. Do not boil.

4 Add lobster tail meat and mix until meat is heated thoroughly.

5 Lay first crêpe flat on the serving dish. Pour ¼ cup of lobster and sauce inside crêpe. Roll up and drizzle with 1 tablespoon of sauce. Repeat with remaining crêpes. Garnish with fresh parsley and serve immediately.

Stewed Okra and Tomatoes

If you love old-fashioned Southern cooking, you'll love this recipe. It's soul food in a crêpe!

4 Servings

- 3 cups of fresh okra, rinsed, trimmed and sliced
- 3 medium tomatoes, peeled and chopped
- 2 slices of bacon, chopped
- 1 small onion, chopped
- ¼ cup of vegetable juice
- 1 tsp of salt
- ½ tsp of black pepper
- 4 basic crêpes

1 First, make crêpes. If you made your crêpes ahead of time, wrap them in foil and reheat in a 325-degree oven for about 10 minutes or until warmed.

2 Sauté bacon in a medium skillet until crispy. Add onion and cook until softened and slightly caramelized.

3 Add okra, tomatoes, juice, salt and pepper and reduce heat to low. Cover pan and simmer for 15 minutes or until okra is tender.

4 Lay first crêpe flat. Spread ½ cup of okra-tomato mixture across the center of the crêpe. Roll up. Repeat with remaining crêpes.

Coq au Vín Crêpes

This recipe is based on the traditional French peasant dish of Coq au Vin, which is now one of the most popular dishes in the world.

4 - 8 servings

- 2 pounds of boneless breast chicken tenders (about 16 pieces)
- 6 slices of bacon
- 2 tbsp of butter
- 3 tbsp all-purpose flour
- 3 cups good red wine
- 2 tbsp of tomato paste
- 1¾ cup of chicken broth
- 2 garlic cloves, minced
- 2 cups of button mushrooms, quartered
- 4 large carrots, diced
- 2 onions, diced
- 2 tbsp of fresh thyme leaves, chopped
- 1 bay leaf
- 1 tsp of salt
- ½ tsp of black pepper
- 8 basic crêpes

1 Fry the bacon in a large skillet until crisp. Remove from pan and place on paper towels. Drain off all but 2 tablespoons of bacon grease. Season chicken with salt and pepper on both sides. Brown chicken in grease until golden brown (about 2 minutes on each side). Remove and set aside.

2 Melt butter in pan. Add carrots, onions, and garlic and sauté until softened and slightly caramelized (about 3 minutes). Add the mushrooms and garlic and sauté for 2 more minutes. Reduce heat, sprinkle the flour over vegetables and stir. Continue to cook for an additional 2 minutes, stirring constantly.

3 Add stock, wine and tomato paste to pan, stirring well to dissolve flour. Crumble reserved bacon and add it, thyme, bay leaf, and reserved chicken to pan. Stir together and let simmer on low heat for 30 minutes, adding more wine if necessary. After it has cooked, adjust seasoning by adding a sprinkle more of salt or pepper to your taste. Remove bay leaf.

4 Meanwhile, if you made your crêpes ahead of time, wrap them in foil and reheat in a 325-degree oven for about 10 minutes or until warmed.

5 Lay the first crêpe on the serving dish. Put two chicken tenders inside the crêpe along with ¼ cup of vegetables and sauce. Roll up and drizzle with two tablespoons of vegetables and sauce. Repeat for remaining crêpes.

Crêpes Coq au Vin: with this meal you will impress your guests because you serve two classical French meals at once.

Zucchíní and Carrot Crêpes

For a light brunch, try these tasty and colorful crêpes with fresh zucchini and carrots cooked inside.

4-8 Servings

- Basic crêpe batter
- ¼ cup of fresh zucchini, grated
- ¼ cup of fresh carrots, grated
- 2 packages of cream cheese, softened
- 1 tbsp of chives, minced
- 1 tbsp of fresh parsley, chopped
- 1 tbsp of fresh dill, chopped

1 First, make basic crêpe recipe. Refrigerate batter for at least 30 minutes.

2 After batter has been refrigerated, add zucchini and carrots and stir until completely incorporated. Now, make crêpes. Cover to keep warm while you make the filling.

3 As you pour the batter across the pan, try to sprinkle the zucchini and carrot strips evenly across the surface of the crêpe.

4 Beat cream cheese for 1 minute until smooth and creamy. Add herbs and mix until thoroughly combined.

5 Lay first crêpe flat on the serving dish. Spread with 2 tablespoons of herbed cream cheese. Fold in half and then into quarters. Repeat with remaining crêpes. Serve immediately.

Chicken á la King in Crêpes

While the original dish was served over toast points, we think that the creamy chicken filling and crêpes is a match made in heaven.

6 servings

- 2½ cups of diced cooked chicken
- 2 tbsp of butter
- ½ cup of chopped green pepper
- 2 tbsp of all-purpose flour
- ½ tsp of salt
- ⅛ tsp of white pepper
- 2 cups of evaporated milk
- 1½ cups of chicken broth
- 1 tbsp of sherry
- 1 4-oz. jar of chopped pimentos, drained
- 6 Basic crêpes

1 Melt butter over medium heat in a medium skillet. Add green pepper and sauté until softened, about 3-4 minutes.

2 Add flour, salt and pepper and stir, cooking until flour is absorbed and mixture is smooth and golden. Add milk, sherry and broth gradually, and cook for an additional 10 minutes, whisking constantly.

3 If you made your crêpes ahead of time, now is the time to wrap them in foil and reheat in a 325-degree oven for about 10 minutes or until warmed.

4 Add chicken and pimentos to skillet, cooking until chicken is thoroughly heated.

5 Ladle ½ cup of chicken and sauce over the first crêpe. Fold in half and then in quarters. Repeat with remaining crêpes and serve immediately.

Crab Benedict Crêpes

Seafood for brunch? Why not? These easy crêpes will keep you satisfied well until dinner.

4 servings

- 4 eggs
- 1 cup of cooked crab meat, crumbled
- 4 basic crêpes
- Hollandaise sauce, see recipe below
- Salt and pepper to taste
- Fresh chives, chopped

Hollandaise Sauce

- 3 egg yolks
- 4 tbsp of butter
- 6 peppercorns
- 3 tbsp of white vinegar
- Salt and white pepper
- 1 tbsp of chopped dill (optional)

1 First, make crêpes. If you made your crêpes ahead of time, wrap them in foil and reheat in a 325-degree oven for about 10 minutes or until warmed.

2 Poach eggs by pouring each one into a skillet filled with simmering water (brought to a boil and then reduced to a simmer). Swirl the egg white with a fork over the yolk so that it doesn't float away. After all of the eggs are placed in the water, let simmer for 6 minutes, or until yolks are cooked to your preference.

3 Meanwhile, make Hollandaise sauce. Combine vinegar and peppercorns in small saucepan over medium heat. Bring to a simmer and reduce to 1 tbsp of liquid. Remove peppercorns.

4 Melt butter. Set aside. Place yolks in blender and mix on highest speed. Through the hole in the lid, with the blender still set on high, slowly stream in the reduced vinegar and butter to the eggs. The mixture will thicken into the consistency of cream. Season with salt and white pepper. Keep your sauce warm by placing it in a double boiler over a saucepan of hot water.

5 Lay first crêpe flat. Spread half of the crêpe with ¼ cup of crabmeat. Fold crêpe in half and then once more, into a triangle. Repeat with remaining crêpes.

6 Remove your cooked eggs from the water and drain on a paper towel. Blot the tops to remove the excess moisture. Place one egg on top of each crêpe and top with 2 tablespoons of warm hollandaise sauce. Season with salt and pepper; garnish with 1 tsp of chives and serve immediately.

Broccoli Au Gratin Crêpes

Use as an easy side dish or on its own as a meatless and satisfying main dish.

8 Servings

- 2 crowns of broccoli
- 1 head of cauliflower
- 1 tsp of salt
- ½ tsp of black pepper
- ½ cup of grated mild cheddar cheese
- 3 tbsp dried bread crumbs
- Cheddar Cheese sauce
- 8 basic crêpes

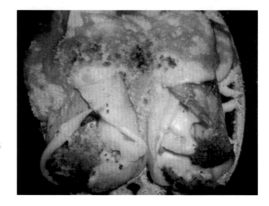

Cheddar Cheese Sauce
- 3 tbsp of butter
- 4 tbsp of flour
- 2½ cups of milk
- 1¼ cups of grated mild cheddar cheese
- 1 tsp of salt
- Pinch of white pepper

1 Wash broccoli and cauliflower. Trim into ½-inch pieces. Place veggies in a large pot of boiling water. Cook for 8 minutes or until tender.

2 Meanwhile, make cheese sauce. Melt the butter in a medium saucepan over medium heat. Whisk in the flour after the butter has melted. Cook for 1 minute, whisking constantly so that mixture does not burn.

3 Heat milk. Add milk gradually to saucepan. Bring mixture to a boil and continue to whisk until it is smooth and thick. Reduce heat and simmer for 2-3 additional minutes. Add cheese and seasonings and stir until combined. Set sauce aside.

4 Once broccoli and cauliflower are cooked, drain vegetables and season with salt and pepper. Preheat oven to 450°.

5 Lay the first crêpe inside an oiled baking dish. Add ¾ cup of vegetables to the inside of the crêpe. Top with 2 tbsp of cheese sauce and roll up. Repeat with remaining crêpes. Once all crêpes have been assembled in the baking dish, pour remaining sauce over top of crêpes. Bake for 10 minutes or until topping turns golden brown

Grilled Portobello Mush-rooms and Tomato Pesto

Enjoy unique crêpe fillings? You'll love the trio of unusual flavors in this meatless main dish.

8 Servings

- 4 large portobello mushroom caps
- ¼ tsp of salt
- ⅛ tsp of black pepper
- 2 tsp minced garlic
- ¼ cup of olive oil
- 8 oz. of sun dried tomato pesto
- 8 oz. of feta cheese
- 8 basic crêpes

Tip: Soaking your mushrooms briefly in water before grilling yields moist and succulent mushrooms.

1 First, make crêpes.

2 Clean mushrooms by wiping caps free of any dirt. To ensure that mushrooms do not dry out while grilling, soak for 3 minutes in a large bowl of water.

3 Meanwhile, mix together olive oil, garlic, salt and pepper. Pat mushrooms dry and brush mixture on top of mushrooms and let them marinate for 5 minutes. Heat grill to medium high heat.

4 Place mushrooms on grill, to the side and away from the center. Grill on each side for 3 minutes, watching to make sure that mushrooms do not burn. Remove from grill and slice each mushroom into ¼-inch strips.

5 Lay first crêpe flat on the serving dish. Spread 1-2 tbsp of pesto across surface of the crêpe. Top with 4-5 pieces of mushroom and sprinkle with 1 tbsp of cheese. Fold top over and then fold again into quarters. Repeat with remaining crêpes and serve immediately.

Asparagus Crêpes with Cheese Sauce

Another reason to love fresh asparagus!

4 Servings

- 2 tbsp olive oil
- 1 tbsp of butter
- 2 cups of white mushrooms, quartered
- 1 lb of thin asparagus
- ½ tsp of salt
- ¼ tsp of black pepper
- ¼ cup of parsley
- 4 basic crêpes
-

Swiss Cheese Sauce
- ⅓ cup of white wine
- 2 tbsp of milk
- 2 tbsp of cornstarch
- 1½ cups of heavy cream
- ¼ teaspoon of salt
- Pinch of white pepper
- ½ cup of grated Swiss cheese
- ¼ cup of grated parmesan cheese
- Pinch of nutmeg

1 First, prepare the Swiss cheese sauce. Dissolve cornstarch in milk. Set aside. Pour wine into a medium saucepan and bring to a boil. Reduce to 1 tbsp.

2 Remove from heat and stir in milk-cornstarch. Add cream, salt and pepper. Stir and let simmer for 2 minutes. Add cheeses and whisk together until melted. Simmer for 1 minute. Remove from heat and stir in nutmeg. Transfer sauce to a double boiler to keep warm while you make your crêpe filling.

3 Next, prepare the asparagus. Bend each piece of asparagus to form a "U" shape. When the asparagus breaks, keep the portion with the tip and discard the stump or cut end. This step will ensure that you have the tenderest part of the asparagus. Next, cut off the tips and cut the remaining stalk into two-inch pieces.

4 Melt butter in large saucepan over medium heat. Add oil once butter melts. Add mushrooms and sauté until mushrooms begin to brown. Sprinkle with salt and pepper. Add asparagus and sauté, adding a little more butter and oil to the pan if necessary. Remove from the heat when the asparagus begins to caramelize (about 3 minutes).

5 Lay each crêpe flat on the serving dish. Add ½ cup of the mushrooms and asparagus. Top with ¼ cup of the Swiss cheese sauce and a sprinkle of parsley. Repeat with remaining crêpes and serve immediately.

Chicken Marsala Crêpes

With boneless chicken tenders, you can have this delicious dish on the table in just 45 minutes.

4-8 Servings

- 2 pounds of boneless breast chicken tenders (about 16 pieces)
- 2 tablespoons of olive oil
- 2 tablespoons of butter
- 2 garlic cloves, minced
- 2 cups fresh mushrooms,
- 2 shallots, diced
- 1½ cups Marsala wine
- 1½ cups chicken broth
- 1 tablespoon fresh thyme leaves, chopped
- 1 tablespoon of cornstarch
- 1 tsp of salt
- ½ tsp of black pepper
- 8 basic crêpes

1 Melt olive oil and butter in a large skillet over medium high heat. Sauté chicken tenders until golden brown (about 5 minutes on each side). Remove chicken from pan and set aside.

2 In the same pan, sauté mushrooms and shallots until mushrooms are caramelized and shallots are translucent. Add garlic and thyme, stir to combine, and cook for an additional minute. Add salt and pepper.

3 Deglaze the pan with the wine and one cup of chicken broth. Combine remaining broth with the cornstarch in a small bowl. Add to pan and bring to a boil. Reduce heat to low and simmer until sauce thickens, about two minutes. Add chicken back to pan and cover. Cook for 15 minutes longer, stirring occasionally.

4 Lay first crêpe flat on the serving dish. Put two chicken tenders inside the crêpe, along with 2 tablespoons of mushrooms and sauce. Roll up and drizzle with one tablespoon of sauce. Repeat with remaining crêpes. Garnish with fresh parsley and serve immediately.

SWEET CRÊPES

Tiramisu Crêpes

Creamy Mascarpone filling in chocolate crepes with chocolate sauce.

6 Servings

- 3 egg whites
- 3 egg yolks
- ½ cup of sugar plus 2 tablespoons, divided
- 8 oz. tub mascarpone
- 1 tbsp of strong coffee
- 2 tbsp of cognac
- ¼ cup of cocoa powder
- Chocolate sauce recipe
- 6 chocolate crepes
- whipped cream and grated chocolate for garnish

Chocolate Sauce
- 8 oz. of semisweet chocolate morsels
- 3 tablespoons of unsalted butter
- ¾ cup heavy cream
- 1 tablespoon of orange liqueur or dark rum (optional)

1. Mix egg yolks, mascarpone, coffee, sugar and cognac in large mixing bowl. Beat 3 minutes. Add mascarpone and beat for 5 minutes more. Set aside.

2. Whip egg whites together. Once the whites have formed soft peaks, add remaining 2 tablespoons of sugar. Continue beating until stiff peaks form. Add to mascarpone mixture and fold until combined. Chill mixture for 1 hour.

3. Now, proceed with making your chocolate sauce. Fill the bottom of a double-boiler with water. Bring to a boil. Place morsels and butter in top bowl. Stir frequently. When mixture is melted, stir in heavy cream with wire whisk. Add liqueur. Blend with whip.

4. Lay first crepe flat on serving dish. Spoon or pipe ¾ cup of mascarpone filling across the center of the crepe. Dust with 1 tsp of cocoa powder and roll up. Repeat with remaining crepes. Spoon hot sauce over the crêpes. Serve immediately.

Strawberry Mousse Crêpes

There's no better way to enjoy the flavor of fresh strawberries than this easy mousse recipe in crêpes.

4 Servings

- 1 envelope of plain gelatin
- ¼ cup of cold water
- 1 tsp of strawberry or raspberry liqueur or extract
- 2 drops of red food covering
- ½ cup of granulated sugar, divided
- 2 cups of washed (stems removed) and sliced fresh strawberries
- 1 cup of whipping cream
- Extra whole berries and whipped cream for garnish
- 4 basic crêpes

1 Add water to gelatin in small saucepan over low heat. Stir until gelatin is dissolved (about 1 minute).

2 Pour strawberries, gelatin-water mixture, ¼ cup of the sugar, extract and food coloring into a blender. Purée until berries are incorporated into the mixture. Pour into a medium bowl and chill for one hour.

3 Whip cream and remaining sugar on low until sugar is absorbed. Raise speed to high and whip until soft peaks form. Fold whipped cream into strawberry mixture and chill for 1 hour to set.

4 Lay first crêpe flat on the serving dish. Spoon or pipe ¾ cup of mousse across the middle and roll up. Repeat with remaining crêpes. You may chill these crêpes for up to 6 hours before serving or serve immediately. Garnish with whipped cream and a sliced strawberry before serving.

Tropical Fruit Crêpes

A refreshing treat and one of our easy dessert recipes that is sure to take you to a warmer climate with the very first bite!

6 Servings

- 2 kiwi fruit, peeled
- ½ cup of diced pineapple
- 1 mango or 2 navel oranges, peeled
- 10 fresh strawberries
- ½ cup of blueberries
- 1 tblsp of lime juice
- 1 tsp of lime zest
- 2 tsp of honey
- ½ cup of toasted coconut
- ½ cup of toasted macadamia nuts
- 1 tablespoon of fresh mint leaves, chopped
- 6 wild berry crêpes

White Chocolate Sauce
- 2 white chocolate baking or candy bars, 4 oz. each
- ¾ cup heavy cream
- 1 tablespoon of orange liqueur (optional)

1 Chop kiwi, pineapple, mango and strawberries into ¼-inch pieces. Combine with blueberries. Add lime juice, honey, zest and mint and coat fruit well. Put in refrigerator and let chill for 10 minutes.

2 Meanwhile, make chocolate sauce and keep warm over double-boiler.

3 Fill the bottom of a double-boiler with water. Bring to a boil. Break up chocolate bars and place in top bowl. Add cream and stir together until melted. Stir in liqueur. Remove fruit from refrigerator. Drain well.

4 Lay each crepe on the final serving dish. Spoon ½ cup of fruit mixture into each crepe and roll up. Drizzle with one tablespoon of warm white chocolate sauce and garnish with 1 tablespoon each of toasted coconut and macadamia nuts. Repeat with remaining crepes. Serve immediately.

Irish Coffee Pudding in Chocolate Crêpes

If you like the smooth flavor of Irish whiskey and the rich flavor of coffee, you'll love this treat.

4 Servings

- 2 pkgs. of instant vanilla pudding mix (3.5 oz each)
- 4 tsp of instant coffee granules
- 1 cup of cold milk
- ⅔ cup of cold water
- 6 tbsp of Irish whiskey
- 1¾ cups of whipping cream, divided
- 8 oz. semi-sweet morsels
- 3 tbsp of butter
- 1 tbsp of rum
- 4 chocolate crêpes

1 Beat pudding mix, instant coffee and milk together in a medium bowl on high speed for 1 minute. Add water and whiskey and beat for another 1-2 minutes until fluffy.

2 In another bowl, whip 1 cup of cream until soft peaks form. Fold into pudding-whiskey mixture and chill for at least 5 minutes or until set.

3 Meanwhile, make the chocolate crêpe batter. Heat milk gently in a small saucepan. Add chocolate. Stir gently until chocolate is melted. Combine chocolate-milk mixture and remaining ingredients into blender and process until smooth. Refrigerate for 30 minutes.

4 Make chocolate crêpes and set aside.

5 To make chocolate sauce, fill bottom of double-boiler with water and bring to a boil. Place morsels and butter in top bowl. Stir frequently. When mixture is melted, stir in remaining ¾ cup of cream with whisk. Add rum and blend with whisk. Place in refrigerator to chill.

6 Lay first crêpe flat on the serving dish. Spoon or pipe ½ cup of filling across the middle and roll up. Repeat with remaining crêpes. Refrigerate for up to 8 hours. Right before serving, drizzle with chocolate sauce and if desired, garnish with whipped cream and mint.

Pear Crêpes with White Chocolate Sauce

The white chocolate sauce complements the sweet taste of the pears and makes it a true delight.

4 Servings

- 4 pears, peeled, cored, and halved
- ½ lemon

- 2 tbsp of butter
- ¼ cup of light brown sugar
- ½ cup of apple juice or cider
- ½ tsp of allspice
- 2 tbsp of dark rum (optional)
- White chocolate sauce
- ¼ cup of toasted walnut pieces
- 4 scoops vanilla ice cream
- 4 basic crêpes
-

White Chocolate Sauce

- 2 white chocolate baking or candy bars, 4 oz. each
- ¾ cup of heavy cream
- 1 tablespoon of orange liqueur (optional)

1 After peeling, coring, and halving pears, rub all sides with the lemon half. Set aside.

2 Melt butter in large skillet over medium heat. Add brown sugar and allspice and stir until dissolved. Reduce heat to a simmer and add apple juice.

3 Place pears in skillet, flat edges down. Cook for 15 minutes and then turn over and cook for an additional 10 minutes or until pears pierce easily with a fork. A golden caramel sauce will form as the pears cook.

4 Meanwhile, make crêpes. If you made your crêpes ahead of time, wrap them in foil and reheat in a 325-degree oven for about 10 minutes or until warmed.

5 Now you can make your white chocolate sauce. Fill the bottom of a double-boiler with water. Bring to a boil. Break up chocolate bars and place in top bowl. Add cream and stir together until melted. Remove from heat and stir in liqueur.

6 After pears are cooked, remove from pan and place on cutting board. Add rum to skillet, and stir it into the caramel sauce. Let simmer for an additional minute. Remove from heat. Cut each pear half into 3 slices. Return pears to skillet and coat gently with sauce.

7 Lay first crêpe flat on a plate. Ladle six pieces of pear over crêpe and 2 tbsp of pear-caramel sauce. Roll up crêpe. Top with one scoop of ice cream and drizzle with 1-2 tbsp of white chocolate sauce. Finish with a sprinkle of walnuts. Repeat with remaining crêpes and serve immediately.

Dessert Crêpes with Fresh Plums

Simmered in a sauce of brandy, apple juice, and ginger, plums make a tantalizing topping for warm dessert crepes.

4 Servings

- 4 tbsp of butter
- 4 tbsp of brown sugar
- 4 peeled and sliced fresh plums (stones removed)
- 4 tbsp of brandy
- 2 cups of apple juice
- ¼ tsp of fresh minced ginger
- 3 tsp of cornstarch dissolved in ¼ cup of water
- 8 basic crepes

1   Melt butter in a medium skillet. Add brown sugar and stir to combine.

2   Add brandy. Cook for 1 minute. Stir in apple juice, ginger and plum slices.

3   Simmer for 10 minutes on low heat until plums are tender. Add cornstarch-water mixture and stir until thoroughly incorporated. Let simmer for 2 minutes until sauce is thickened.

4   Place two warm dessert crepes on each plate. Ladle 5-6 plum slices and ¼ cup of sauce over each serving. Serve immediately.

Peach Melba Crêpes in Raspberry Sauce

This recipe is based on the classic dessert created in honor of the soprano Dame Nellie Melba.

4 Servings

- 4 fresh peaches, peeled
- ½ cup of canola oil
- 2 tbsp of cinnamon sugar
- Raspberry sauce
- Vanilla ice cream
- 4 basic crêpes

Raspberry Sauce
- 1 cup of fresh or frozen raspberries
- 2 tbsp of orange juice
- ¼ cup of seedless raspberry jam
- 2 tablespoons of sugar

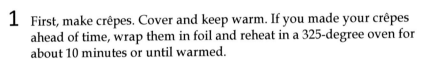

1 First, make crêpes. Cover and keep warm. If you made your crêpes ahead of time, wrap them in foil and reheat in a 325-degree oven for about 10 minutes or until warmed.

2 Preheat grill or grill pan to medium heat. Cut peeled peaches in half and remove stone. Brush cut edge of peaches with canola oil and sprinkle with cinnamon sugar. Place cut edges on grill. As first side cooks, coat the other side of each peach with more oil. Grill for 3-4 minutes until visible grill marks appear. Turn peaches over and grill the remaining side for 3 more minutes. Remove from heat and sprinkle with remaining cinnamon sugar. Slice each halve into 4 slices for a total of 32 peach slices.

3 Purée the raspberries and orange juice in a blender. Strain to remove seeds. Pour mixture into a small saucepan and add ½ cup seedless raspberry preserves and sugar. Heat just until mixture comes to a boil and then simmer 2-3 minutes.

4 Lay first crêpe flat across serving platter. Spoon 8 slices of peach inside crêpe. Roll up and top with one scoop of ice cream. Drizzle with raspberry sauce. Repeat with remaining crêpes. Serve immediately.

Chocolate Mousse Crêpes with Raspberries

Although rich and full of chocolate flavor, this easy chocolate mousse filling is as light as air.

4 Servings

- 2 tbsp of orange liqueur
- 3 tbsp of sugar
- ½ cup of semi-sweet chocolate chips
- 2 cups of heavy whipping cream
- 2 egg whites
- 4 chocolate crêpes
- 1 cup of fresh raspberries
- Chocolate sauce

Chocolate Sauce
- 8 oz. semi-sweet morsels
- ¾ cup of heavy cream
- 3 tbsp of butter
- 1 tbsp of rum (optional)

1   Stir together sugar and liqueur in small saucepan. Place over medium heat and bring to a boil. Remove from heat and stir until sugar is dissolved. Set aside.

2   Make chocolate sauce. Fill the bottom of a double boiler with water. Bring to a boil. Place morsels and butter in top bowl. Stir frequently. When mixture is melted, stir in heavy cream with wire whisk. Add optional liqueur. Stir together until glossy and smooth. If necessary, you can reheat gently in microwave.

3   Using electric mixer, beat egg whites until stiff peaks form. Fold cooled chocolate mixture into whites. Set aside and beat the remaining whipping cream until soft peaks form. Fold chocolate-egg white mixture into cream until thoroughly combined. You may chill for up to 24 hours.

4   Lay first crêpe flat on the serving dish. Pipe ½ cup of mousse across crêpe. Sprinkle with fresh raspberries. Now, roll up and repeat with remaining crêpes. Next, drizzle each crêpe with chocolate sauce.

Crêpes Suzette

This classic dessert is the perfect combination of sweet and tangy.

4 Servings

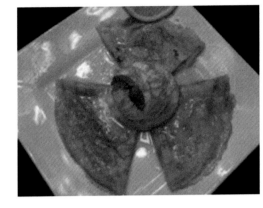

- 12 basic crêpes
- 4 tablespoons butter
- ¼ cup sugar
- Juice of 6 oranges; zest from one
- Extra whole orange for garnish
- 3 tablespoons of orange liqueur (We use Grand Marnier)
- 3 tablespoons cognac (optional)
- 12 basic crêpes

1 Melt butter in large skillet over medium heat. Stir in the sugar, zest, juice, and liqueur. Stirring constantly, reduce sauce to ⅔ cup.

2 Very delicately add each crêpe to the pan—one at a time—and coat it in the sauce. (We used a fork rather than a spatula for this.)

3 Fold each one in quarters, and arrange three on each plate, repeating until each crêpe has been dipped and plated. You may overlap them or arrange in a circle as we did in the picture above, with a scoop of ice cream in the middle and extra sauce over the top. Scrap up the extra bits of orange zest and add orange slices as your garnish.

4 *Adults only:* If you wish to flambé the sauce, reserve two tablespoons of orange liqueur and add three more of brandy.

5 Stir together and remove the pan from the heat. Ignite with a match and pour the flaming sauce over the crêpes.

6 Important Note: You should only ignite the sauce using a metal pan; do not use a non-stick pan. Please exercise due caution and remove all flammable materials (dishcloths, etc.) from the work area.

Lemon Curd and Blackberry Compote

Hmmm. The perfect dish that is refreshing and sweet at the same time.

8 Servings

- 2 tbsp of lemon zest
- ½ cup of fresh-squeezed lemon juice
- 1½ cups granulated sugar
- ½ tsp of salt
- 6 tbsp of butter
- 3 eggs
- Blackberry compote
- Fresh lemon slices,
- Whipped cream
- 8 basic crêpes

Blackberry Compote
- 2 pints of fresh blackberries
- 2 tbsp of sugar
- 2 tbsp of lemon juice

1 Stir together berries, juice and sugar in a small bowl. Crush half of berries. Stir mixture and let chill for about 2 hours, until a juice forms. Meanwhile, make crêpes. Cover and keep warm.

2 Whisk together lemon zest, juice, salt and sugar in a saucepan over medium heat. Bring to a boil, lower heat and simmer 5 minutes. Next, add butter to lemon mixture. Stir together until butter melts. Remove mixture from heat and let cool to room temperature (about 20 min).

3 In a separate bowl, beat eggs lightly. Add to lemon mixture until well blended. Return to heat and cook over medium-low heat, stirring constantly, for an additional 10 to 15 minutes or until mixture thickens and coats spoon. Do not let mixture boil.

4 Remove mixture from heat. Pour curd through a fine sieve into a bowl. Cover with sheet of plastic to keep a skin from forming. Chill until set.

5 Lay first crêpe flat on serving plate. Spread ¼ cup of curd across the crêpe. Fold in quarters. Top with 2 tablespoons of compote. Top with whipped cream and lemon slice, if desired. Repeat and serve.

CRÊPES FOR SPECIAL OCCASIONS

Mini-Crêpes Filled with Chicken Salad

Mini-Crêpes are the perfect party appetizer and can be used as finger food.

30 Mini-Crêpes

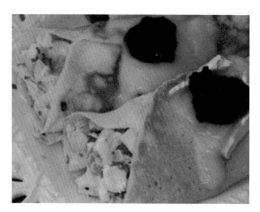

- 3 cups of cooked chicken, diced into ¼-inch pieces
- ⅓ cup of mayonnaise
- ¼ cup of diced sweet onion
- ¼ cup diced celery
- 1 tsp of lemon juice
- 1 tsp of sugar
- ½ tsp of salt
- ¼ tsp of black pepper
- 1-inch squares brie cheese
- ½ cup of whole cranberry sauce or relish
- tbsp of fresh chopped parsley
- 10 6-inch basic crêpes

1 Stir together mayonnaise, lemon juice, sugar, salt and pepper in a medium bowl. Add onion, celery, parsley and mix well. Finally, add chicken and stir together until chicken is moist and coated with the dressing.

2 Preheat oven to 350 degrees.

3 Lay first crêpe inside an oiled 9" x 13" baking dish. Fill crêpe with ⅓ cup of chicken salad. Roll up. Top with one square of brie. Repeat with remaining crêpes.

4 Place baking dish inside preheated oven. Bake for 10 minutes or until brie melts.

5 Remove from oven and top each crêpe with 1 tsp of cranberry sauce. Serve immediately.

Christmas Crêpe with Peppermint Filling

Especially Kids love this chocolate crêpe with peppermint filling. The red-white candies radiate Christmas spirit.

4 Servings

- 2 blocks of cream cheese, softened (8 ounces each)
- ¼ cup of sugar
- 1 tbsp of vanilla
- ¼ cup of crushed hard peppermint candy
- Whipped cream for garnish
- 4 chocolate crêpes

Chocolate Sauce

- 8 oz. of semisweet chocolate morsels
- 3 tablespoons of unsalted butter
- ¾ cup heavy cream
- 1 tablespoon of orange liqueur or dark rum (optional)

1 First, make chocolate crêpes. You will need four crêpes for this recipe. Cover and keep warm while you mix the crêpe filling.

2 Break the peppermint candies (except 4) by hand into pieces or put into a dishcloth and crush with a hammer.

3 Mix cream cheese, sugar, and vanilla with electric mixer until smooth. Next, stir in crushed candies.

4 For the chocolate sauce: Fill the bottom of a double-boiler with water. Bring to a boil. Place morsels and butter in top bowl. Stir frequently.

5 When mixture is melted, stir in heavy cream with wire whisk. Add optional liqueur. Blend with whip.

6 Lay first crêpe across serving platter. Spoon ¼ cup of cream cheese filling across half the crêpe. You may roll in half or in quarters as pictured. Garnish with whipped cream and top with a whole candy for decoration. Serve immediately.

Tres Leches Crêpes for Valentine Day

Tres Leches is a traditional Venezuelan dessert. With Crêpes and strawberries it makes a truly romantic Valentine's dessert.

2 Servings (3 Crêpes each)

- 1½ cups all-purpose flour
- 4 tbsp melted butter
- 12 oz. of evaporated milk
- 3 eggs
- 1 tablespoon granulated sugar
- pinch of salt
- 1 tablespoon of vanilla
- 1 cup of sweetened condensed milk
- Whipped cream
- 1 cup of diced strawberries
- 6 basic crepes

1   Melt Butter in a small pan. Combine melted butter, flour, condensed milk, eggs, granulated sugar, salt, and vanilla sugar into a blender and mix until well-blended.

2   You may also combine them by hand. If combining by hand, mix the eggs and milk separately and combine slowly with the dry ingredients. Mix in the melted butter last.

3   Refrigerate the batter for at least 30 minutes. This gives the batter the opportunity to rest and fully come together.

4   Now prepare your crêpes.

5   Fold first three crêpes into quarters and arrange in a circle on serving dish. Drizzle with 2 tbsp of sweetened condensed milk. Top with a dollop of whipped cream and 2 tbsp of diced fresh strawberries. Repeat with remaining crêpes and serve immediately.

Crêpe Croque-Madame

This easy brunch recipe is based on the French Sandwich "Croque Monsieur" and a heavenly start for your Easter holiday.

4 Servings

- ½ cup of sour cream
- 1 tbsp of Dijon mustard
- 2 tsp of garlic powder
- 8 slices of very thinly sliced deli-quality ham (We used Virginia baked ham)
- 1 cup of grated swiss cheese

- 2 eggs, fried sunny-side up, to your preferred level of doneness
- 4 basic crêpes
- salt and pepper, to taste
- Parsley, chopped, for garnish

1 First make your crêpes.

2 Mix together sour cream, mustard and garlic in a small bowl.

3 Lay first crêpe flat on a working serving. Spread 1 teaspoon of sour cream mixture across bottom of crêpe. Top with 1 tbsp of cheese. Fold in half. Spread top of crêpe with 1 tsp of sour cream mixture. Cover with 1 more tablespoon of cheese. Move crêpe to a foil-lined baking sheet. Repeat with remaining crêpes.

4 Place baking sheet under broiler until cheese melts and begins to brown. Remove from oven and keep warm while you prepare the eggs.

5 Make sunny-side-up eggs in a medium pan according to your taste.

6 Once eggs are done, top each folded crêpe with one egg and sprinkle with salt, pepper, and parsley garnish. Serve immediately.

Vegetarian Crêpe with fresh Veggies

If you love Pasta Primavera, then you'll devour this Vegetarian Crêpe.

6 Servings

- 1 tbsp of butter
- 1 tbsp of vegetable oil
- 1 shallot, chopped
- 1 clove of garlic, minced
- 1 lb. asparagus spears, cut into 1-inch pieces
- 1 medium yellow squash, sliced and quartered
- 1 medium red bell pepper, seeded and julienned
- ½ cup of vegetable broth
- ⅓ cup of green peas, frozen
- ½ cup of shredded parmesan cheese
- salt and pepper to taste
- ¼ cup of chopped fresh parsley
- 6 savory crêpes

1   First, make crêpes and cover to keep warm. If you made your crêpes ahead of time, wrap them in foil and reheat in a 325-degree oven for about 10 minutes or until warmed.

2   Melt butter in a large skillet over medium heat. Add shallots and sauté until transparent and softened, about 2 minutes. Add garlic and cook for an additional minute, stirring constantly.

3   Add oil, asparagus, squash and pepper. Sprinkle with salt and pepper. Sauté just until squash and pepper have softened and asparagus is crisp-tender, about 4-5 minutes. Deglaze pan with vegetable broth. Add peas and stir together until liquid is absorbed and peas are heated through. Remove from heat and add parsley, stirring to combine.

4   Lay first crêpe across serving platter. Spoon ⅓ cup of vegetables across half the crêpe. You may roll in half or in quarters as pictured. Dust crêpe with 1 tbsp of parmesan cheese. Repeat with remaining crêpes and serve immediately.

Made in the USA
Middletown, DE
15 July 2017